THE AMERICAS

Paul Manias & Fiona May

FAMILY LIBRARY
of
WORLD TRAVEL

Statue of Liberty, New York *previous page*. Standing majestically on Liberty Island stands the 151-foot-high Statue of Liberty. In an extravagant gesture, the French presented her to the people of America in recognition of their long friendship. It is reached only by ferry, from which some of the best views of both the statue and New York City are to be seen.

Niagara Falls *this page*. Rising from the turbulent mist of Niagara Falls the arc of a rainbow can be seen above the world's most famous waterfalls. Newlyweds still flock to see this natural wonder, confirming it as 'Honeymoon Capital of the World.' This dramatic spectacle of water plunging 200 feet can be appreciated from various vantage points including walkways, boats, cable cars and helicopters.

First published in 1985
for AGT Publishing
by Octopus Books Limited
59 Grosvenor Street
London W1, England

© 1985 Octopus Books Limited

ISBN 0-933521-14-6

Produced by Mandarin Publishers Ltd
22a Westlands Road
Quarry Bay, Hong Kong

Jacket Photography: Zefa Picture Library

CONTENTS

Machu Picchu, Peru. The Andes have long kept the secret of Machu Picchu, 'Lost City of the Incas,' and its history remains shrouded in mystery. Discovered in 1911 by the US senator Hiram Bingham, it is one of the finest remaining examples of the Inca civilization.

INTRODUCTION

Traversing almost the entire scope of latitudes between the Arctic and Antarctic regions, the Americas span the complete spectrum of climate and landscape. Their vast area is formed into two massive continents, each unique, each full of contrasts, each an adventure.

The Americas derive their name from the Florentine explorer, Amerigo Vespucci, once wrongly credited with the discovery of the North American mainland in 1497. Christopher Columbus, seeking to confirm his belief in a spherical world, had preceded Vespucci by five years. The native Indian civilizations, however, had been in existence for as many as 20,000 years prior to this 'discovery' – the Inuits in the frozen tundra of the north, the tribes of the North American mainland, the Mayan and Aztec cultures of Mexico, and the extraordinary Incas of South America.

Canada's magnificent alpine scenery, among the most beautiful and dramatic in the world, remains untouched. Much of it has been designated national parkland and is protected for the enjoyment of all who wish to take advantage of this national heritage. Communing with nature is a popular pursuit among Canadians, a pastime that visitors will be eager to share.

Across the border lies the United States of America, as diverse in its landscape, climate and people as the rest of the Americas combined. Bathe in Californian sunshine or ski down a glacier in the Rocky Mountains – the recreation possibilities are endless.

The people of the USA originate from all corners of the globe. American identity is many-sided, an extraordinary tapestry of cultures; and the country that fostered a pioneering spirit still provides numerous opportunities to pursue a wide variety of beliefs and ambitions. Gregarious and friendly by nature, the American people, with their zest for living, extend a warm welcome to visitors.

Further south and into the sunny tropics lies Mexico, a land of curious contrasts where the ruins of an ancient world merge with the style and tempo of today. The beautiful beaches, fringed with palms and washed by turquoise seas, attract thousands of visitors in search of sun, the same sun that was worshipped as a god by the ancient Mayan and Aztec civilizations. Mexico will seduce your senses with the aromas of spicy food, the taste of tropical fruit, the brilliant colors of the festival costumes and a kaleidoscope of bright flowers.

Though linked by a narrow isthmus and sharing a name with the northern continent, South America is a very different and fascinating world. Exploring South America will take you to the extremes of climate and terrain – from steamy Amazonian jungle to misty mountain peaks in the Andes or to the exotic beaches of Brazil. Your adventure will take you to the 'Lost City of the Incas' on a mountain top not far from the Peruvian capital of Lima, a city of gracious colonial architecture and lush garden suburbs. And to Buenos Aires, capital of Argentina – an elegant city with a European flavor and atmosphere. Rio de Janeiro on the Brazilian coast is synonymous with the rhythm and beat of Latin America, while fast-moving Rio is the chic and exciting playground of South America.

The excitement felt by the European explorers who discovered the Americas is felt today by travelers from all over the world.

The Capitol, Washington DC. The Capitol is the forum for the Senate and the House of Representatives, and the cradle of the US government. It is of classic design and appropriately grand proportions, and is crowned by Thomas Crawford's Statue of Freedom. A city ordinance protects its position as the tallest building in Washington, while the splendor of The Mall and the Washington Monument before it ensures it as a focus of attention.

—THE UNITED STATES OF AMERICA—

New York • Washington
Connecticut • Boston • San Francisco
San Diego • Las Vegas

The Statue of Liberty, sentinel of the United States of America, bears the words 'Give me your tired, your poor, your huddled masses yearning to breathe free . . .' – the open greeting of the 'land of the free.' Freedom is what the country is all about: an individualism treasured since the United States won their independence from the British.

The USA spans the entire spectrum of climate and landscape from the arctic tundra of Alaska to the tropical paradise of Hawaii, and from the arid deserts of Death Valley to the verdant forests of New England. More cosmopolitan than that of any other country, its enormous immigrant populations maintain many traditions from their countries of origin, while uniting in a national identity of which all Americans are proud.

The amazing natural wonders of this great country, such as Niagara Falls and the Grand Canyon, are paralleled by the great achievements of its people. From bringing the fantasy of space travel to reality at Cape Canaveral to creating a wonderland of makebelieve in Disneyland, America is a land where dreams come true.

'Get up and go,' the phrase that encapsulates the energy and enthusiasm of the American people, can also be adapted as an inspiration for exploring the 'Pandora's Box' of things to see and do in the USA. What better place to start than in its cities?

New York is a place where even the most worldweary traveler comes alive in the electric atmosphere. The grandiose art deco spires of the Empire State Building and the Chrysler Building contrast with the sleek towers of the World Trade Center, and contribute to that famous and strangely beautiful skyline which holds such a fascination for travelers. The archetypal all-night city, New York pulsates with life and excitement 24 hours a day; its frenetic pace will make a deep impression on every visitor. Also memorable are the treasures in its many museums, notably the Guggenheim Museum and the Museum of Modern Art. The best way to see New York City is by walking around the various areas – Greenwich Village, Soho, the South Street Seaport, Central Park, the Upper West Side – and trying to absorb some of the excitement and activity for which New York is so famous.

By contrast, Boston's pace is slower and more gracious. One of America's most historic cities, it is the place where the 'Fathers of Independence' instigated the revolution against the British. Boston is the largest city in New England, and the perfect starting point from

Brooklyn Bridge, New York *left.* For more than one hundred years New Yorkers have made their way between Brooklyn and Manhattan via the Brooklyn Bridge. It is a curious mixture of styles, with its Gothic arches on two large supports trussed together with an intricate web of steel cables encasing a wooden walkway (now a popular jogging path). The bridge spans over 6,500 feet at a height of 133 feet, and a stroll across it will provide excellent views of Manhattan's skyline.

9

Manhattan skyline, New York City
above. A world-famous sight and the subject of countless photographs, Manhattan's skyline is still as awesome as it was in the 1930s when the tallest buildings were the two splendid art deco skyscrapers, the Empire State Building and the Chrysler Building. Today they have been dwarfed by the twin towers of the World Trade Center, from which you can get a bird's-eye view of New York. For an even more exciting look at the skyline it is possible to take a helicopter tour over the city.

which to enjoy this very special part of the USA. The unspoiled beaches of Maine, the picturesque farming villages of Vermont and New Hampshire, and the forest glades of Connecticut have a magical mood and atmosphere. Steeped in history, New England is the birthplace of modern America.

Westward we arrive at the Great Lakes and, of course, the Niagara Falls which, annually, draw thousands to view the spectacle of cascading water. Lying on the shores of Lake Michigan, Chicago (dubbed 'Windy City') is the second largest metropolis in the USA and a major commercial center. A city of superlatives that include the tallest building (Sears Tower) and the busiest airport in the world, it is also recognized for its patronage of the arts.

West across the prairies lie the glorious natural wonders of Montana's national parks, particularly Yellowstone and Glacier National Park – the latter noted for its spectacular Rocky Mountain scenery.

Tiffany & Co., New York *below*. On fashionable Fifth Avenue in midtown Manhattan is Tiffany and Company, one of the world's most famous jewelry stores. Featured in the film *Breakfast at Tiffany's*, starring Audrey Hepburn, Tiffany's has long been synonymous with the exotic and expensive. Among its collections of luxury items are works by Paloma Picasso that range from $400 to $60,000, and a yellow diamond weighing in at 128.5 carats and selling for a mere $1,000,000. Novelty gifts, however, are available at reasonable prices.

Central Park, New York *left*. A green oasis in Manhattan's maze of skyscrapers, Central Park is the largest recreational area in New York. During the day the park is brimming with people seeking a haven from the frenetic pace of the city. A labyrinth of paths twist and weave through the park, popular with joggers and cyclists alike. Other attractions are the zoo and a boating pond. Central Park also provides the venue for numerous concerts of both classical and popular music.

Faneuil Market, Boston *right*. Close to Boston's City Hall and adjacent to the historic meeting house of Faneuil Hall stands Faneuil Market. Yellow and green canvas canopies fill the side halls with light and color that fall on the multitude of stalls and trolleys full of enticing treats, paintings and souvenirs. The market began in 1826 and was reopened in 1976 after extensive restoration. Overflowing onto the surrounding walkways, a profusion of flower stalls and little sidewalk cafés make a colorful picture, while strolling entertainers gather their audience from the browsing shoppers.

Mystic Seaport, Connecticut *left.* The romance and adventure of New England's seafaring past come alive in the lovingly recreated 19th-century port and village at Mystic. Set on the banks of the Mystic River and lined with tidy rows of old buildings, the 17-acre village is home for a community of artisans and craftworkers. The Mystic Seaport Museum includes four historic ships and a working shipyard. Demonstrations are given in the art of rigging, sailmaking and furling. There are also exhibits of model ships and a scale model of Mystic Seaport.

New England foliage *above.* The forest becomes a mosaic of autumnal colors as the leaves pass through their seasonal change, from green to red, rust or gold and finally brown. With the fading warmth of summer the lush green forests of New England shed their leaves in a final glorious show of color. The rustling leafy carpet underfoot announces the coming of winter. The magic of New England is best felt during the crisp clear mornings of early October before the oranges and browns of autumn give way to the white of the winter snows.

Buckingham Fountain, Chicago *right*. Buckingham Fountain, set in Grant Park near Chicago Harbor, is a symphony of water streaming from jets and cascading over tiers. Its Renaissance appearance contrasts with the ultra-modern skyscrapers of Chicago's business world. The 'Windy City' fosters a policy of conserving its architectural heritage, particularly its public squares, these are a forum for the arts, with many sculptures and impromptu performances of Chicago's street theater groups. The squares also provide a popular lunchtime retreat for office workers.

Mount Rushmore National Monument, South Dakota *below.*
About 25 miles south of Rapid City, the stone images of four of America's most revered presidents – Washington, Jefferson, Theodore Roosevelt and Lincoln – are set into Mount Rushmore. They were the dream of Grutzon Borglam, who was inspired by the large bare granite face in South Dakota's Black Hills. His fourteen-year struggle to sponsor and complete the work was finally achieved in 1941. The herculean task of removing 450,000 tons of rock was achieved by gradually drilling and chipping the surface away to form the four faces, each over 60 feet high.

The Space Needle, Seattle *left.*
Making a surreal sight against a backdrop of office-block lights that seem suspended in space stands the futuristic Space Needle, over 600 feet high. An elevator will whisk you up to the observation deck and restaurant in a mere 45 seconds. From the top you can enjoy fabulous views of Seattle and the surrounding area. The tower was constructed as a major feature in the 1962 World's Fair staged at the Seattle Center. The Center's 74 acres house numerous recreational and cultural facilities, including the Pacific Science Center and the Seattle Art Museum Pavilion.

Beyond the Rockies, on the northwest coast, stands the modern city and port of Seattle. Its colorful pioneering past includes the development of its lumber industry and the gold fever which swept through it in the mid-19th century. It remains the chief access point for Alaska.

Going south, Oregon is a shangri-la of natural treasures protected by a strong policy of conservation. It contains no less than thirty state parks and possesses one of the most scenic coastlines in the world.

San Francisco manages to combine natural and manmade beauty in a colorful picture which includes a glorious bay, forest parks and imaginative buildings and bridges. Its extroverted, charismatic personality has a unique way of entertaining. Here we find the 'flower child' sub-culture of Haight Ashbury, the charming artists' colony in Sausalito and the lively areas of Chinatown and Fisherman's Wharf.

Dorothy Parker described California's other major city, Los Angeles, as '72 suburbs in search of a city.' A vast urban expanse incorporating the familiar names of Santa Monica, Pasadena, Beverley Hills and of course Hollywood, LA is literally a conglomeration of places, each with a very different flavor. Browse through the exclusive boutiques on Rodeo Drive in Beverley Hills or stroll in the Bohemian markets of Venice Beach. Los Angeles will never be short of something different for you to see or buy. Hollywood's fading glory has been replaced by the splendor of Bel Air's palatial houses while Westwood, scene of many an extravagant movie première, still glows with the neon of its picture palaces. No visit to Los Angeles is complete without a visit to Disneyland, a playground for 'children of all ages.'

Some 2,500 miles off the California coast lies the tropical paradise of the Hawaiian Islands, a haven for sun-worshippers. Out of 132 islands only six are open to tourism, the most popular being Oahu, with Hawaii's capital Honolulu and the famous Waikiki Beach. Oahu is the most sophisticated of the islands, with international resorts, luxury hotels and fine restaurants. If you are seeking something more tranquil, then the islands of Maui and Kauai are garden paradises of lush vegetation, hibiscus and frangipani blossoms, pineapple groves and dramatic scenery.

Back on the mainland and by contrast to the luxuriant Hawaiian Islands, Las Vegas stands as a neon oasis in the Nevada Desert. Much of the central southern area of the USA is arid and studded with cacti.

Mount McKinley, Alaska *above.*
Glistening in the morning sun stands the breathtaking summit of Mount McKinley. Nearly as high as the Himalayan peaks, Mount McKinley reaches 20,000 feet and was called 'Denali' ('High One') by the Athabascan Indians. The double peaks of Mount McKinley have posed a climbing challenge since the early 1900s and should be attempted only by experienced climbers. The mountain is the highlight of Mount McKinley National Park which is the second largest park in the USA and is noted for its wildlife.

Waikiki Beach, Hawaii *right.* Waikiki Beach on Oahu has some spectacular surf; with such gigantic waves it's not surprising that surfboard riding originated here. The local Hawaiians first used long wooden planks to ride the mountainous sea. Today Waikiki is still popular with surfers, their boards now small and made of fiberglass, but it has become a favorite spot for the less energetic as well. Its beautiful palm-lined sandy beach is packed with sun-seekers. Set back from the beach are some of the best hotels, restaurants and nightlife to be found on the islands.

Across the Nevada state border and into Arizona lies one of nature's finest sculptures – the Grand Canyon, an enormous chasm plunging a mile down to the powerful Colorado rapids. Southeast of the canyon, the artistic hand of nature has created a surreal work in the Petrified Forest of Arizona. A staggering 200 million years old, this former forest of ferns and conifers, that now stand as pillars of stone, bears all the colors of an artist's palette. To the north lies the Painted Desert, a gallery of abstract stone forms, the color and mood of which changes as the sun crosses the sky.

Everything about Texas, 'The Lone Star State,' is BIG but, as its name (taken from an Indian word meaning 'friends') suggests, the people of Texas will give every visitor a warm welcome. Its two major centers of Houston and Dallas are large, thriving cities that reflect the wealth of Texas's oil and cattle industries. Houston is the name the world remembers for those nailbiting moments when Neil Armstrong first walked on the moon. With special permission it is possible to arrange to see the Mission Control Center.

If Houston represents the future, then New Orleans is a reminder of the past. It is an enchanting city, particularly in the French Quarter, with its 200-year-old cobbled streets lined with a mixture of Spanish and French-style buildings, their balconies trimmed with lacy wrought iron. The open-air cafés and the French Market have a European ambience; the air is rich with the enticing aroma of Creole dishes wafting from the many restaurants. The air is also alive with music – Dixieland jazz,

Merced River Valley, Yosemite National Park, California *below.* Of all Yosemite National Park's many natural features, perhaps the most striking is the glorious Merced River Valley. Its shimmering waters are overlooked by El Capitan, the world's largest single outcrop of granite. To the right are the Bridal Veil Falls, casting a mist over the towering sequoias that line the river banks. In the 1,200 square miles of Yosemite National Park there are numerous other astounding sights, notably Yosemite Falls, at 2,425 feet the highest in the world.

Golden Gate Bridge, San Francisco. San Francisco's most famous landmark is often almost hidden by fog. The bridge is actually red, not gold as its name implies. The enormously long span linking San Francisco with the Northern Bay Shore reaches across the gap in the coastal ranges known as the Golden Gate, hence the bridge's name. The bridge was completed in 1937, some six months after San Francisco's other major bridge, the Oakland Bay Bridge, was opened. The road section is some 220 feet above the bay and the bridge's towers reach up to 746 feet.

Cable car, San Francisco *right.* The hills of San Francisco are a daunting prospect for any pedestrian and the cable cars provide a welcome relief from the climb as well as an enchanting ride. The colorful old carriages, which have undergone an extensive restoration program, are a must for any visitor to San Francisco. As you trundle up the steep ascents to the tune of the conductor's bell, the magical city comes into view: the Victorian houses perched precariously along the hilly streets, the spectacular bridges spanning San Francisco Bay – usually dotted with sailboats – and the island of Alcatraz (upper right) with its now-defunct prison.

Cajun music and, as Shrove Tuesday approaches, the non-stop cacophony of the Mardi Gras celebrations.

Florida, 'Sunshine State', lives up to its reputation. Its subtropical climate is perfect for growing the citrus fruit for which it is famous. An ideal retreat from the harsh winters of the north, Miami is typified by palm-studded beaches, azure seas and lavish hotels which cater for the thousands who come annually to enjoy the sun.

Off the western coast of the peninsula lies a sprinkling of some 40 islands that comprise the Florida Keys, harboring some of the prettiest seascapes in the USA. Each of the keys sets its own pace: some are placid little fishing villages, others are lively resorts. Florida has more to offer than just lying on beaches, however. The Everglades are a maze of waterways and mangrove swamps that form the habitat for some of the world's rarest birds and reptiles. The manmade wonders include Cape Canaveral, launch site for many space explorations and home to the Airforce Space Museum.

Center for the government, Washington has risen from the muddy squalor of its early development and fulfilled the ambitious vision of its French designer, Major Pierre L'Enfant, who elevated it to the status of a splendid capital. The focus of the city falls on its two most important buildings – the White House and the Capitol, linked by the ceremonial boulevard of Pennsylvania Avenue. The city's many fine buildings and monuments leave a lasting impression of grandeur and stately beauty.

Sampling the variety of food available in the different parts of the USA is an exciting part of any tour. 'Fast foods' are available everywhere for those in a hurry, but so are delicious regional and ethnic specialties.

New York has perhaps the finest collection of ethnic styles of cuisine anywhere in the world – a *smorgasbord* of flavors. In San Francisco your tastebuds will be seduced by excellent seafood and its famous 'surf 'n' turf,' while in Los Angeles' Japanese sushi bars the fashion is to eat your seafood raw.

Marina, San Diego *below.* Set between the rich blues of sea and sky, a forest of yacht masts pinpoint the boat marina of San Diego known as the 'Harbor of the Sun'. Across the bay the modern skyline of the city is visible. San Diego is thought to have the most ideal climate in the USA, and there are plenty of sights to satisfy even the most jaded tourist: the San Diego Zoo, Balboa Park, Coronado Island, the beaches, the missions, Sea World – the list goes on and on.

Las Vegas *right.* A beacon in the desert, glowing 24 hours a day with neon light, Las Vegas is unquestionably the world capital for gambling. A haven for insomniacs, Las Vegas has everything to keep a visitor entertained at any time of the day or night – international celebrity acts, lavish cabaret and risqué shows. But gambling is the main attraction – from the 'one-armed bandits' to the concentration and tense silence of the blackjack tables and the climactic roar of a big win on the 'craps' table. Fortunes can be made or lost within the space of a few hours, and frequently are.

Bryce Canyon, Utah *above.* The steep rock walls of Bryce Canyon reveal 60 million years of geological history. In its curious shapes and gorgeous colors one can visualize the form of grand castles, ancient temples and cathedrals in a wondrous chasm 9,000 feet deep. Best seen in the early morning light the canyon's magical aura is enchanting. Although the 34-mile drive around the perimeter offers spectacular views, some of the best vantage points can only be reached on horseback or on foot.

For a complete alternative the Hawaiian luaus can be a veritable feast and in New Orleans the rich Creole and Cajun dishes of jambalaya and gumbo filé – delicious, spicy and aromatic – make excellent use of the area's fine seafood. If unusual seafood is to your taste then Florida's conch chowder and turtle steaks will be a special treat, as will Key Line pie. If you're after traditional dishes, then Texas steaks and New England clam chowder are not to be missed.

Wherever you venture and whatever you see and do when exploring the USA, you can be assured that there is always something new and exciting awaiting you.

Monument Valley Navajo Tribal Park, Arizona *below.* A surreal gallery of strange sculptured shapes fills Monument Valley in Arizona. The park has a collection of *mesas* and *buttes*, broad flat tables of rock that rise above the landscape, as well as deep canyons. As the day passes into dusk, the changing color of the massive rocks provides a haunting backdrop for the countless Hollywood westerns filmed in this area. For modern-day travelers not astride a horse, the park offers a scenic but slow-going drive.

Minerva Terrace, Yellowstone National Park *left.* Appropriately named after Minerva, the Roman goddess of the arts, Minerva terrace is a natural phenomenon of exquisite beauty. Situated in Yellowstone, the first and largest of the national parks in the USA, the terrace's tiers of rock are bathed in the steamy flow of minerals from the hot springs that surge from under the ground. Deposits of the minerals calcify to form pink and white layers – a fairytale staircase. Yellowstone has a plethora of natural phenomena, including 10,000 geysers and a mountain of black obsidian (volcanic glass).

Grand Canyon, Arizona. For all its mighty scale the Grand Canyon's beauty is its most impressive feature. Layers of exposed rock chronicle two billion years of geological history in a picture book of reds, yellows, browns, grays and blues. The sheer proportions are staggering. The canyon stretches for 277 miles and the river has gouged a path as wide as 16 miles in places. From the high vantage points that bring it into view, the Colorado River seems a modest trickle, but a mile down between the exposed cliffs of the canyon, one can appreciate how its savage torrents have achieved this herculean feat of nature.

Corn dance, New Mexico *right.* The elaborately decorated headdress of the Pueblo Indians of New Mexico add more than a splash of color to the ritual of the corn dance. Their intricately embroidered costumes and flowing red plumes make a colorful display in this most important of Indian ceremonial dances. The Pueblos perform their carefully choreographed dances to bring rain, cure illness and to celebrate their fertility rites.

Street jazz, New Orleans *above.* The streets of New Orleans swing to the rhythm of music. Every May the city plays host to the New Orleans Jazz and Heritage Festival, a celebration of the music form that was born in the back streets of the city. Ragtime, blues, traditional and Dixieland jazz, folk and gospel music fill the air. Impromptu 'jam' sessions capture the improvisatory nature of all the jazz styles. The traditional garb for the musicians includes bowler hat, bow tie and a striped vest.

Walt Disney World in Orlando, Florida *right.* The dream of Walt Disney to create a fairytale land of joy for 'children of all ages' is realized in Walt Disney World and in its predecessor, Disneyland, in Anaheim, California. Walt Disney World far exceeds the size of its Californian sister but offers similar attractions. The Magic Kingdom alone has more than 40 things to see and do in its Fantasyland, Frontierland, Liberty Square, Tomorrowland, Adventureland and Main Street.

TRAVEL TIPS

The mainland of the United States spans four complete time zones so travelers should take note of local times. For fast travel, the USA has the most comprehensive network of domestic air travel in the world. For more leisurely travel and at an economical price, buses give the visitor an excellent opportunity to see the countryside.

Shoppers will find some excellent regional specialties during a tour of the USA. The northeast has a fine selection of antiques and some bargains for those prepared to hunt around. In the south and southwest, interesting examples of Mexican and Indian arts and crafts are available, while in San Francisco and Hawaii an array of Chinese and Oriental gifts are on offer. Shoppers should note Hawaii's early trading hours from 8:00 am to 4:00 pm.

Although most national holidays are celebrated throughout the country some, such as Memorial Day (last Monday in May) and Columbus Day (second Monday in October), are not acknowledged by all states. The legal minimum drinking age also varies between states from 18 to 21 years old. Some states prohibit the import of liquor.

Tipping is expected when good service is received, with 15% being the norm for waiters and 50¢ the customary tip for small services.

Undoubtedly the best way to see America is by automobile, although the massive distances can take up a large part of the holiday. For those who have the time for touring, the tollways provide fairly uninterrupted traveling with frequent places for service and refreshment. Alternatively, if you are planning to spend time in just one area, it is best to fly and rent an automobile. But remember to check the state and city laws as they vary considerably from place to place.

FARE 10¢ OR A COUPON

Parliament buildings, Ottawa. Set upon a natural throne overlooking the Ottawa River rests the collection of formidable Gothic structures that comprise Ottawa's Parliament buildings. Their stone walls and roofs of green copper make an impressive sight. Peace Tower, which dominates the group, bears a white lamp to signify when Parliament is in session.

CANADA
Ottawa • Toronto • Montreal
Alberta • Québec • Vancouver

Second only to the Soviet Union in size, and occupying two-fifths of North America, Canada's area of just under four million square miles stretches between the Pacific and Atlantic oceans. To the north it is bounded by the Arctic Ocean and to the south it shares its border with twelve American states. It is massively spectacular – from the icy tundra of the north to the warmer south where its people, its industries and its agriculture are heavily concentrated. Everything about Canada's natural landscape is on a grand scale. To the west lie the Rocky Mountains bordered by a coastline carved by ancient glaciers into fjords with spectacular cliffs, many of them over 7,000 feet high. Seemingly endless prairies span much of the center, while to the east lie the Great Lakes. For lovers of the great outdoors, Canada offers a unique experience, but for the less energetic a wealth of culture exists in its modern cities. First inhabited by the Indians, Canada was claimed for France by Jacques Cartier in 1534. Thus began the strong French influence, counterbalanced by the presence of France's long-time rivals, the British. Canada has now emerged as a major independent nation with its own distinctive identity.

Mention Canada and images spring to mind of Mounties in bright red uniforms, of lumberjacks cutting their way through monstrous trees in enormous alpine forests, of salmon and fabulous seafood, and of golden streams of maple syrup dripping over stacks of fresh, hot pancakes. As appropriate as these images are, they give only a partial glimpse of what Canada has to offer – a country of unique scenery and a culture influenced by the many different races that make up its society.

The most obvious influences are French and British. French and English are both official languages in Canada. The contrasting moods of these two cultures are highlighted by the genteel English atmosphere of Victoria in the west, and the French flavor of Québec in the east. In addition to people of French and English extraction there are descendants of the original Indian and Eskimo tribes and more recent immigrant groups from far and wide. The people of Canada are proud of their heritage and try to preserve their diverse cultural identity. The government actively promotes multi-culturism, and so visitors are likely to experience a strong sense of the differences in background together with the warm welcome that is so recognizably Canadian.

Royal Canadian Mounted Police *left.* Proud and hearty, the officers of the Royal Canadian Mounted Police carry on the tradition of the force established in 1873. Wearing bright red jackets, riding boots and those familiar hats, the Mounties still police the law in the Yukon and Northwest Territories. The famous slogan 'A Mountie always gets his man' bears witness to their history as an effective force in one of the most untamed parts of the world. In Regina, Saskatchewan, the Royal Canadian Mounted Police training depot houses a museum devoted to the Mounties, with displays of armory and uniforms.

31

CN Tower, Toronto *right.* Shaped like a rocket, the CN (Canadian National) Tower, the world's tallest freestanding structure, reaches the impressive height of 1,815 feet. Built to provide an aerial mast for telecommunications, the tower doubles as a unique recreational center with its revolving restaurant and lively discotheque. Just reaching the restaurant in glass-sided elevators that draw you up 1,100 feet in under a minute is an exciting experience. On a clear day you can see Niagara and Buffalo Falls from the 'sky pod's' outdoor observation deck.

Notre Dame de Bonsecours Chapel, Montreal *left.* Montreal's oldest church, Notre Dame de Bonsecours, was originally constructed in 1657. Fire destroyed the original building and the church was rebuilt in 1771.

Château Frontenac, Québec *below.* Towering majestically above Québec City stands the massive Château Frontenac. Reminiscent of its French counterparts the enormous château, with its green copper roof and numerous turrets, suggests a palace for royalty. Instead the château is a fine hotel providing superb accommodation. From its commanding position there are some of the best views of the city.

An ideal place to begin experiencing Canada's many facets is Québec City, the oldest seaport in the country and the heart of French Canada. Situated in a commanding position overlooking the St. Lawrence River, it is perhaps the most picturesque of the major centers. The old quarter, with its charming little cobbled streets, its 17th-century stone houses, its French-speaking people and its sidewalk cafés, evokes the atmosphere of France. Little wonder then that the city motto is 'je me souviens' – 'I remember'. Within the confines of the city walls there is much to see and enjoy – by foot or in one of the colorful horsedrawn calèches that wend their way around this lovely old city. Of particular interest is the Citadel where you can watch the pomp and pageantry of the famous Changing of the Guards. Full of history and character, Québec offers you a chance to capture the romance of the past.

Still in Québec province but further inland lies Montreal. One of Canada's largest and oldest cities, it is a place of strong contrasts. The population is predominantly French-speaking, but there is a sizeable English contingent and the atmosphere of this dynamic and charming city is definitely cosmopolitan. There is a curious mixture of old and new; ultra-modern skyscrapers are set against a background of Montreal's quaint Old Town. Underground lies a warren of shopping complexes linked by pedestrian walkways and a near-silent metro system, while above ground the traditional Jewish delicatessens and colorful Chinese shopping district provide interesting alternatives.

A hub for the arts, Montreal boasts two fine galleries – the Montreal Museum of Fine Arts and the Museum of Contemporary Art. Between them they have a notable collection of both old and modern works. The Place des Arts provides one of North America's best venues for productions of opera, theater and ballet and is put to frequent use. The city has a strong association with sports as well as culture, having been the host for the 1976 Olympic Games. Varied and interesting, Montreal is never short of surprises for those who seek out its many treasures.

Moraine Lake, Banff National Park
left. Tucked among the jagged peaks of the Rocky Mountains, laced with trails of snow, lie the icecold waters of Moraine Lake. This, and Lake Louise, are considered to be Banff National Park's most beautiful lakes. The banks of the lake are lined with alpine forests that abound with wildlife. Breathing the fresh mountain air is an invigorating experience, inspiring you to take part in the lake's many sporting pursuits. These include canoeing, hiking and mountain climbing.

Maligne Lake, Jasper National Park
right. Cupped by surrounding peaks that reach to nearly 10,000 feet, Maligne Lake is one of the most popular features of Jasper National Park. Locked within its natural basin the lake sits over 5,000 feet above sea level among the Rocky Mountains. It is the largest glacier-fed lake in the Canadian Rockies. The lake's breathtaking scenery is best appreciated from a cruise boat which sets out every two hours. This trip will give ample opportunity to take memorable photos of this very special part of the world.

Cowboys, Alberta *right.* Canada's pioneering past owes a lot to the cowboys of yester-year, who ventured into new parts of the country to establish the grazing herds for which the Canadian prairies are noted. Those pioneering days are gone but the spirit of the cowboy lifestyle is kept alive on the large ranches and at Canada's many rodeos – showplaces for the cowboys' skills. The largest rodeo in the world takes place annually in Calgary. Known as the Calgary Stampede, it draws thousands to watch and to participate in the exciting and often dangerous events celebrating the cowboy tradition.

Landscape near Calgary, Alberta *left.*
In the soft and golden glow of dawn, the gentle undulations of the Alberta countryside have a serene appearance. Calgary lies near the foothills of the Rockies on the edge of a sweeping expanse of prairieland. The ranches near Calgary are ideal for raising horses, the mode of transport still preferred by the cowboys of these vast lands and by the Royal Canadian Mounted Police, who founded the city in 1875.

Indian chicken dancers *below*. Displaying the colorful plumage of their traditional costumes these two tribal Indians prepare for a demonstration of the 'chicken dance.' For the Indians, dance is an integral part of religious practice and belief; each tribe has its own particular dances and costumes. Dancing is used to invoke magic, cure illness by expelling evil spirits, assure food production, bring rain, pray for good hunting and celebrate the stages of life – birth, puberty and death. The dancers' mimicry of animals reflects the Indian belief that all living things possess a soul.

Mount Eisenhower, Banff National Park *right*. Rising above the icy water of a mountain river is the rocky peak of Mount Eisenhower. The angular shape of its rugged pinnacle, often veiled in swirls of mist, reaches high into the skies over Banff National Park. The scenic park roads that wind their way through this splendid Canadian countryside pass close to this unusually shaped peak and its neighbors, Cascade Mountain and Mount Brett.

Across the border in Ontario and situated on the south bank of the Ottawa River lies Canada's capital city, Ottawa. Small in comparison to Toronto and Montreal, Ottawa was chosen by Queen Victoria to be the capital due to its strategic location at what is virtually the crossroads between the French and English sectors of Canada. Its name originates from that of an Indian tribe, 'Outaowac', which traded guns with the French voyagers of the 17th century.

Now the center for Canadian government, Ottawa is a particularly neat city with a fine mixture of Victorian Gothic buildings and modern office towers. Rideau Canal flows through the heart of the downtown area creating a colorful picture of pleasure boats in the summer, while in the winter skaters glide across its icy surfaces. The city's attractive, neatly tended gardens provide beauty of flower and foliage from spring to autumn. On Parliament Hill the famous bearskinned soldiers in their smart red uniforms perform the majestic daily ritual of the Changing of the Guards. Overlooking them, Peace Tower, some 291 feet high, makes an excellent vantage point from which to take in the splendid views of Ottawa and the river.

Frenetic, cosmopolitan, futuristic, lively and avant-garde, Toronto is the most modern of Canada's cities. Lying on the edge of Lake Ontario it is well situated for the recreational pursuits that attract so many visitors to its shores. The 'brave new world' style of architecture which the city has pursued is complemented by the restoration and conversion of its older buildings which now house fashionable studios and boutiques. The surreal skyline is dominated by the CN Tower, the tallest freestanding structure in the world.

'Please walk on the grass' is Toronto's welcome to visitors to its 15,000 acres of parkland. Among them, Toronto Island Park, a ferry ride across the harbor, has some beautiful gardens and many recreational facilities. Of the city's numerous museums, a few well worth a visit are the Art Gallery of Ontario, renowned for its collection of Henry Moore sculptures, the Royal Ontario Museum, for its ethnological collections, and the Ontario Science Center.

Cradled between the snowcapped mountains that form its backdrop and the bay waters that lap its shores lies Vancouver, the largest city on the west coast. Less than 100 years old, it is a modern metropolis, its center shared by the unusual art deco buildings of yesteryear and today's gleaming new office towers. Once no more than a small papermilling community called 'Gastown,' Vancouver has done much to restore the area of its early settlement. Gastown today is an enchanting quarter full of Victorian buildings and warehouses converted into a host of interesting little shops, atmospheric restaurants, and artisan studios.

Though its origins are mainly British, Vancouver is now home for a large ethnic community including the biggest Chinatown in Canada. Bustling with activity, the district has a colorful market area. The city's favorable climate makes walking a popular pursuit. For this purpose there are many parks, including Stanley Park, noted for its scenic walks and magnificent totem poles.

Situated on the southwest tip of Vancouver Island lies Victoria. First used as a supply center for the Hudson Bay Company, it became the capital of British Columbia in 1871 when the province joined the Canadian Confederation. The city has adopted a very English character, typified by its Victorian and Tudor-style architecture, its shiny red

Yacht marina, Vancouver *above.*
Luxury yachts and pleasure boats
cluster around the jetties of
Vancouver's marinas. Vancouver is
the most important of Canada's
Pacific ports; its ideal weather and
attractive harbor make it a boating
paradise. Little wonder then that
pleasure boats outnumber summer
cottages here! Vancouver has an
impressive maritime history that
began in 1778 when Captain James
Cook mapped the coast. He was
followed by Captain George
Vancouver, after whom the city was
named. Vancouver is also the home
for the famous *St. Roch*, the first ship
to navigate the Northwest Passage.

doubledecker buses and its replica of Shakespeare's birthplace. You
can capture some of the genteel atmosphere by taking traditional
afternoon tea at the Empress Hotel or in the lush surroundings of the
Crystal Gardens' conservatory.

Victoria, too, enjoys a mild climate which aids the cultivation of its
splendid gardens and parks. Perhaps the best example is the Butchart
Gardens, where you will find a variety of attractive areas in the style of
traditional English, Italian and Japanese landscaping. Of Victoria's
sixty parks, its many museums and attractions, one of particular
interest is the Olde English Village, a replica of 17th-century England. It
is even possible for travelers to stay in some of the rooms, which are
furnished in period style.

Away from the cities, much of Canada, particularly in the west and
north, remains wilderness. In order to preserve these quite spectacular
areas, 29 national parks have been established. In these nature reserves
you can spot anything from a large grizzly bear to a porcupine or
mischievous chipmunk. The flora can range from delicate alpine
flowers to thick forests of pine, maple and cedar or hills covered in a
carpet of mountain heather. The oldest and perhaps best-known
reserve is Banff National Park. Picturesque Banff village, tucked
between two enormous mountains, is the major resort of the Rockies.
From the village you can take a gondola up the mountains overlooking

Banff, take a range of hikes, go mountaineering, or take a soothing dip in the hot springs at Sulphur Mountain. One of the park's greatest treasures is Lake Louise; fed by a glacier that glistens in the morning light, its mirror-like surface reflects the majestic surrounding peaks.

More spectacular mountain scenery can be enjoyed at Jasper, one of the largest of Canada's national parks. Located high in the mountains, the park has a wealth of lakes, waterfalls, crevasses and glaciers. At the base of the Athabasca glacier lies the massive Columbia Icefield, the largest accumulation of ice in the Rockies.

With its myriad natural beauties and wilderness to admire and explore, and its cities that vary so widely in character and appearance, Canada is a vast exciting treasure trove for the traveler to discover and enjoy.

TRAVEL TIPS

No passports are required by United States residents along the border, but some identification is necessary. Reciprocal arrangements extend to the currency. However, it is preferred that you exchange your money for Canadian dollars.

A US driver's license is valid in Canada. Fuel comes in liters and distances in kilometers. The national speed limits are 50 mph and 60 mph; traffic signs are often bilingual. With such vast distances you may prefer to take advantage of Canada's efficient air and rail services.

Canada's fine selection of shops stay open until 5:30 or 6:00 pm and until 9:00 pm on Thursdays and Fridays. Banks are open weekdays from 10:00 am to 3:00 pm. If you're dining out or taking a taxi, it is usual to offer a tip of 15%. Porters generally receive 75¢ per bag.

The warmest time to visit Canada is from May to September. The weather grows distinctly cooler in October when autumn colors are at their best. The first signs of snow come in November and cold weather lasts into March and April.

Polar bears, Northwest Territories *below.* Frolicking in the snowfields is a favorite pastime for the polar bears of the Northwest Territories. In the wonderland of snowfields and icy glades, the bears blend so well with their surroundings that only the black tips of their noses and dark eyes can be seen against the white landscape. Feeding mainly on fish, polar bears are cuddly in appearance but ferocious in nature.

Church in Taxco. Typical of the Spanish colonial style of Mexico's village churches is this old chapel with its three-tiered baroque belfry. Taxco is an important religious center for Mexico. Thousands make an annual pilgrimage here for the town's Holy Week festivities at Easter.

MEXICO

Taxco • Mexico City • Teotihuacán
Puebla • Yucatán

Vibrant with color, Mexico is both exotic and mysterious. Civilization has existed here for more than 20,000 years, the most distinctive ancient cultures being those of the Maya and the Aztecs. They were followed by the Spanish, who colonized the country in the 16th century. The mixed descendants of these cultures make up the Mexico of today, a country of warm and friendly people who take great pride in their traditional crafts and festivals – spectacles of costume, music and dance.

Set astride the Tropic of Cancer, Mexico's climate, though generally hot, varies with the terrain. On the coast sun-drenched beaches such as Acapulco are reliably tropical, while inland the capital and many of Mexico's colonial towns enjoy a temperate climate. Mexico is the perfect place to escape the cold North American winter – to relax in the sun, enjoy the nightlife, explore the ancient sites, and simply unwind at a relaxing pace.

Bordered by the US to the north and Belize and Guatemala to the south, Mexico is the most northern of the Latin-American republics. Its 6,000 miles of coastline are washed by the Pacific Ocean to the west and the waters of the Gulf of Mexico and the Caribbean sea to the east. Mexico's mixture of jungle and desert is dominated by a fertile central plateau with lush valleys, snow-capped mountains and thermal springs.

Set like a crown on the plateau some 7,000 feet above sea level lies Mexico City. Originally called Tenochtitlán, Mexico City began when the Aztecs built their capital here, inspired by the sighting of an eagle perched upon a cactus and with a serpent between its jaws. (The sighting fulfilled an ancient prophecy and the eagle and the serpent have since become the national symbols for Mexico, depicted both on its flag and its currency.) The founding of the settlement was a remarkable achievement. The Aztecs created large land areas in Lake Texoco from reeds packed with earth and held together by the roots of trees planted around the perimeters. Gradually their industrious efforts resulted in a series of islands, divided by a network of canals. From these humble beginnings has evolved Mexico City. The city and its surrounding areas have a population exceeding 14,000,000. It is the core of Mexico's political, cultural and commercial life. The afternoon siesta is largely obsolete but the people retain an unhurried approach

Festival of the Virgin of Guadalupe
left. Dancers in brilliantly colored costumes crowned with elaborate plumage perform every year on December 12th at Guadalupe. The festival commemorates the appearance of the Virgin Mary to an Indian peasant in 1531. It is believed that Mary instructed the peasant to build a church on the site; when he reported this to the local priest, he was met with disbelief and so returned to the Virgin for guidance. She instructed him to pick roses from barren ground and wrap them in his cloak. When this had been done, the image of the Virgin appeared on the cloak. These events converted many Indians to Catholicism and the colorful Indian festival celebrates their continuing faith.

43

Mayan stone carving, National Museum of Anthropology *below.* The old and new worlds of Mexico come together in the National Museum of Anthropology in Mexico City. Set in the attractive grounds and gardens of Chapultepec Park, the museum is a striking example of modern architecture. Its comprehensive displays of the pre-Columbian cultures, including the Olmecs, Mixtecs, Zapotecs, Totonacs, Toltecs, Chichimecs, Mayas and Aztecs, make it one of the finest anthropological collections in the world. The exhibits comprise jewelry, ornaments, tapestries and some excellent examples of sculpture and masonry of the early cultures, including this one of Mayan stone carving.

in other ways, and the parks and streets are brimming with those taking their respite from the day's work to watch the world go by. The 'mañana' philosophy rules life less here than in the country's provincial towns and villages but travelers nevertheless need to adapt to the prevalent unpressured approach and to what seems a casual view of punctuality. Once you understand this fundamental difference between Mexico and the time-conscious West, then the best of this fascinating country and its amiable people can be enjoyed.

A good starting point for 'people-watching' is in Mexico City's *zocalo.* The second largest city square in the world, it was once the site of the Aztec ruler's splendid Halls of Montezuma. The Spanish invaders demolished the Aztec city, replacing it with striking examples of Spanish colonial architecture, several buildings of which border the *zocalo* – primarily the National Palace which features murals by Díego Rivera, portraying Mexico's history.

An important aspect of the Mexican way of life is seen in the markets. The daily ritual of buying food is turned into a social event – the markets are a meeting place. To experience the most lively atmosphere go on a

Sunday to La Lagunilla and the adjacent 'Thieves' Market' where you can purchase almost anything. It is customary to haggle over the prices; rarely is anything sold for its initial asking price. The markets are often the venue for street performers, from the traditional organ grinders to clowns and acrobats. In the evening the wandering Mariachi players perform for paying tourists in Garibaldi Plaza.

An insight into Mexico and its people and history is best obtained at the modern National Museum of Anthropology in Chapultepec Park. Acclaimed as one of the finest museums in the world, its comprehensive displays reveal the contrasts in the cultures that comprise Mexico's population and history.

To the north of the capital lie two of Mexico's most important historical treasures. The first is the Shrine of the Virgin of Guadalupe, the second is Teotihuacán, the 'City of the Gods'.

Away from the capital some of the real flavor of Mexico can be sampled in the classic colonial villages and towns. Lively at night, their sleepy afternoons still follow the traditional siesta. Taxco is one such place. It is a prosperous silver-mining town, established upon the discovery of silver here in the early 1500s. Built along a series of terraces that hug the mountainside and connect by a network of narrow cobbled streets and lanes, this picturesque town is a fine example of colonial architecture. Its whitewashed houses with their red-tiled roofs and flowers cascading from every balcony have earned it the status of a national monument. Mexico is noted for its silver and Taxco has a

Floating gardens of Xochimilco *above.* Jostling through the canal area of Xochimilco in Mexico City are dozens of brightly decorated *trajineras*, each one trying to outdo the others with elaborate flower displays.

Kukulkan Pyramid *below.* The ordered geometry of this pyramid dominates Chichén Itzá, center of the Toltec civilization. Dedicated to their serpent god, Quetzalcoatl, it contains a jaguar-shaped throne.

45

Stone carving, Temple of Quetzalcoatl, Teotihuacán *above.* The puzzling mystery that surrounds the ancient 'City of the Gods', Teotihuacán, and the sudden disappearance of its people, remains unsolved. Covering several square miles, the city is dominated by the awesome Pyramid of the Sun. At one end of the two-mile-long Avenue of the Dead stand the remains of the Pyramid of the Moon. At the other end of the avenue is the most outstanding of Teotihuacán's buildings, the Temple of Quetzalcoatl, ornately decorated with stone carvings including the head of the serpent god Tlaloc.

Temple of the Sun, Palenque *right.* Screened by dense jungle, the ancient city of Palenque remains one of the finest examples of the Mayan civilization. It is dominated by the Temple of the Sun, set on its commanding altar and housing a stone mask of the curious Jaguar Sun. Among the city's other superb temples, the Temple of the Foliated Cross bears an uncanny resemblance to temples in southeast Asia. In the Temple of the Inscriptions lies the tomb of the Palenque ruler; the crypt, ornately decorated in jewels and jade, is a splendid sight.

Church of San Francisco Acatepec, Puebla *far right.* On the outskirts of the picturesque colonial town of Puebla stands the majestic village church of San Francisco Acatepec. Entirely covered with *azulejos* (glazed tiles) of rich blues and sparkling golds, the intricate and lavish ornamentation of the facade glistens in the sun like treasure.

profusion of shops selling the wares of its numerous silversmiths.

Equally beautiful is Puebla, founded by the Spanish in 1531. It looks out onto the twin snowcapped volcanoes of Popocatepetl (Smoking Mountain) and Ixtaccihuatl (Sleeping Lady). Famous for ceramics, which adorn many of the town's buildings, Puebla is also noted for the ornate domes and facades of several of its sixty churches. But for those who just want to partake in the easy pace of the village, then the shady town square with its cafés and bandstand makes the ideal location to do as the Mexicans do: sip coffee and forget your woes.

Oaxaca, 'The Jade City,' lies in a valley surrounded by high mountains. Although dominated by colonial buildings the town is a center for Indian culture and has a unique and bustling Indian market. Oaxaca has some splendid baroque churches and is a good starting point for some of Mexico's most magnificent archaeological ruins, especially Monte Alban.

Another colonial town noted for its peaceful old plazas, which abound in tropical flowers and fountains, is Guadalajara. Genteel and gracious it reflects much of Mexico's old-world charm. With its many architectural treasures, museums and atmospheric markets it is a must for travelers in Mexico.

The capital of the Yucatán is Merida, 'the White City', so named for its many white and pastel buildings. It lies in the center of the peninsula in what was the heart of the Mayan civilization. From here some of the earliest Mayan cities, many screened by thick jungles, reveal the splendor and majesty of what is the zenith of this culture's architecture.

Mexico has some of the most beautiful beaches in the world; some of the best are located on the Yucatán peninsula. Soft white sandy beaches make it a haven for sunbathing while underwater a wonderland of coral forms the second largest reef in the world, teeming with tropical fish – a scuba-diver's paradise.

In contrast to the quieter beaches of the Caribbean, the Pacific Coast has some of Mexico's liveliest resorts, particularly the legendary Acapulco. Chic and sophisticated, it has long been a popular

destination for the jet set who soak up the sun by day and seek out its pulsating nightlife after dark.

Set on one of the world's most beautiful bays backed by palm trees and mountains, Acapulco has everything one could want from a beach holiday – with seas that range from pounding surf to tranquil waves, and coves that provide a host of water sports, including fishing. There's never a dull moment, especially when the famous Quebrada divers plunge from the cliff tops into the swirling sea below or the *Voladores* perform the ancient ritual of the flying pole dance.

Closer to the Tropic of Cancer is Puerto Vallarta, a popular resort which manages to retain its Mexican character and fishing village atmosphere. As well as its beautiful beaches it has become a haven for sea-angling contests and scuba diving. Some seven miles south is Mismaloya, an unspoiled beach paradise that formed the set for John Huston's *Night of the Iguana*.

Sampling the food of Mexico can be a real adventure. The Indian, Spanish and French influences on the country's cuisine mean that there is a wide variety of tastes to enjoy and savor. The favorable climate and fertile lands provide Mexico with a cornucopia of exotic fruits and vegetables. There are at least 60 types of chili alone, ranging from hot to sweet. A surprising number of commonplace foods in our diet originated in Mexico, including tomatoes, potatoes, avocados, pineapples, vanilla, chocolate and even turkeys. But perhaps the most significant food is corn; it forms the basis for tacos, tortillas, tamales and enchiladas.

Chichén Itzá, Yucatán *left.* Once a peaceful Mayan settlement, Chichén Itzá was conquered by the Toltecs who built their grand structures on the ruins of the early Mayan site. The photograph depicts the Temple of the Warriors. Its columns, in the form of serpents, provide an example of the most advanced form of pre-Columbian art. The temple sits atop a tiered pedestal, at the base of which stand the Group of a Thousand Columns, believed to have been the market place.

Icacos Beach, Acapulco *left.* Acapulco provides tourists with a choice of 23 sun-drenched beaches on which to laze away the afternoon. Some, like La Condessa, are chic and popular, the shore crowded with the lithe, tanned bodies of the jet set. By contrast Icacos offers a quieter retreat; its sweeping arc of sandy beach is washed by the tranquil waters of Acapulco Bay. It is a safe swimming area and ideal for most water sports.

Butterflynet fishing on Lake Patzcuaro *below.* The pace of life on Lake Patzcuaro is gentle. The local fishermen of the island of Janitzio set out onto the placid lake waters as did their forefathers with graceful gossamer nets that resemble butterflies. From their dugout canoes the fishermen deftly dip their nets into the water and lift out their catch of whitefish, which are later sold to the lakeside restaurants. The charming ritual of using the nets is often demonstrated to visitors by fishermen on the dockside.

In addition to the national dishes of *paella*, *molé sauce* and a range of rich soups, travelers to Mexico will have the chance to try regional delicacies such as the turtle soups of Baja or Acapulco's fish salad. Colorful and aromatic, the food is always interesting. The fiery sauces deserve to be treated with respect – and to help cool those fires are some of the finest beers in the world. For those seeking something a little unusual there is an array of tropical fruit drinks and colorful cocktails, or perhaps tequila served with salt and a wedge of lime. However you choose to quench your thirst, it's worth avoiding the local water and the consequent wrath of the infamous 'Montezuma's revenge'.

Mexico has long been associated with sunny days on tropical beaches, lazy afternoons dozing under the shade of a sombrero and hot spicy foods and luscious fruits. Indeed all this awaits every visitor, but for the intrepid, an Aladdin's cave of ancient civilizations, cities and art is there to be discovered.

TRAVEL TIPS

US citizens planning a stay in Mexico need a tourist card, obtainable at consulates or border crossing stations. Take a passport, birth certificate or some other form of identification. If you plan to drive, a US driver's license is valid, but additional insurance is essential, as is a car permit. Mexico's highway speed limit is 60 mph.

A good alternative way to see the country is by rail, especially on the scenic line through Copper Canyon. Taxis are plentiful, but the fare should be settled first for those without meters. Outside most of the large hotels, bilingual taxi guides are available to show you the sights.

Wherever you go it is wise to be wary of Mexico's strong sun.

49

Christ the Redeemer, Rio de Janeiro.
Casting a blessing over Rio de Janeiro, the 120-foot-high statue of Christ the Redeemer stands 2,300 feet up on Corcovado Mountain. It was constructed in the 1920s and paid for by donations made to churches all over Brazil. Spectacular by day, the statue is even more striking at night when it is illuminated. To reach the summit of Corcovado you either catch an open-sided cog railway train or go by a road which passes several lookout points and picnic spots.

A vacation in South America is an adventure. It is a continent of unique wilderness with fascinating customs and intriguing cultures. With the bewildering fauna of the Galapagos Islands, the frenetic nightlife of Rio, the impenetrable jungles of the Amazon and untamed mountains of the Andes with their lost cities, traveling in South America is a spellbinding experience.

The land is vast and diverse in its terrain and its people, and travelers can get a taste of the differences in the continent by visiting the three major cities: Rio de Janeiro in Brazil with its sun-blessed beaches; Lima, capital of Peru and the base for exploring the Inca culture; and Argentina's Buenos Aires with its European atmosphere.

The glory of the Inca civilization thrived in its isolation until the 16th century when the Spanish conquerors ravaged the Inca cities and plundered their wealth. Very few cities survived the onslaught. Of those remaining, Machu Picchu is a breathtaking reminder of the achievements of the Incas.

Rio de Janeiro welcomes its visitors with the open arms of Christ the Redeemer, the world-famous statue that stands on its lofty altar at the peak of Mount Corcovado. At the foot of the mountain lies a myriad of natural treasures: fifteen miles of glorious shoreline consisting of tiny coves and vast stretches of powder-white beaches, a stunning bay of deep blue waters studded with small islands, and the unusually shaped 'Sugarloaf Mountain' – landmark of Rio.

With such a beautiful setting it is little wonder that Rio has become an international playground noted for its carefree, hedonistic atmosphere. The locals, known as *cariocas*, have an infectious fun-loving approach to life that culminates annually in the world's most famous party – Carnival. Officially lasting for the five days up to Ash Wednesday, but with a build-up of several weeks, Carnival is an exuberant spectacle of color, music and samba.

The 24-hour pursuit of pleasure in Rio begins on its famous beaches – Copacabana and Ipanema. Synonymous with Rio, Copacabana is the heart of the city's resort area, a $2\frac{1}{2}$-mile stretch of sandy beach brimming with sun-seekers. Bordering the beach, Avenida de Atlantica is lined with fine hotels, sidewalk cafés, glamorous shops and numerous antique stalls.

Rio has many lovely parks and gardens for those seeking a respite from the sun and sand. The Botanical Gardens are especially noted for

The gates of Lima Cathedral *left.* Bordering on the Plaza des Armas, the cathedral is built on the site of the original cathedral destroyed in one of Lima's devastating earthquakes. The present building was constructed in the early part of the 18th century. Passing through the massive iron gates you reach the main entrance. To the right is a small chapel containing the remains of Lima's founding father – Pizarro. Some particular features include splendid carved choir stalls, presented as a gift by King Charles V, and striking silver altars.

Women spinning wool, Peru *right*. A frequent sight high up in the mountains around Puno are small groups of Indian women chatting as they spin the rough wool fibers into yarn for knitting. Their constant spinning uses the wool fibers of alpaca, llama and, with recent farming efforts, vicuna. Puno is renowned for the quality and cheapness of its woollens, particularly the thick ponchos that shield against the severe cold of the area. Apart from the ponchos some fine sweaters, socks and scarves can be purchased as well as the unusual woollen animal toys known as *animolitos*.

Traditional Peruvian costume *below*. Set against the peak of Huayna Picchu that towers over the Inca city of Machu Picchu, this colorful pair are dressed in the traditional costumes of this region. The style of weaving dates back to the pre-Columbian origins of the Indian culture. Its motifs of birds, flowers and trees pay reverence to the Indians' harmonious existence with nature. The elaborately embroidered saucer-like hats are peculiar to this part of Peru, but the earflaps featured on the man's hat are also common in Bolivia's cold mountain areas.

their enormous water-lilies and vast array of exotic orchids. Apart from its flora, the city has some splendid sights. The most popular is Sugarloaf Mountain, which can be reached by glass-sided cable car. From the summit are some of the most superb views of Rio and its unique setting. For different perspectives, take a trip to Paqueta Island, one of the prettiest of the eighty or so islands in Guanabara Bay, or venture into Tijuca Forest, which offers a tropical paradise of waterfalls, bright flowers and forest walks.

One of the world's leading exporters of gemstones, Rio's shop windows and stalls glitter with a colorful array of aquamarine, tormaline, amethyst and topaz jewelry. Some of the city's many gem workshops offer guided tours. The most elegant and fashionable boutiques can be found in the streets bordering Ipanema Beach. On Sundays the Hippie market has a good selection of local artifacts.

Rio's restaurants cater for nearly every ethnic taste, but for something Brazilian, try *feijoada*, the national dish consisting of black beans simmered in a variety of meats and served with rice and green vegetables. Be sure also to try the national drink *guarana*, made from the seeds of an Amazonian fruit.

Lima is Peru's capital, and the gateway to some of the most dramatic archeological sites in the world. Established in 1535 by the Spanish conqueror, Pizarro, Lima was originally known as 'The City of Kings' and was for many years the center of the western hemisphere's development. The city straddles the Río Rímac, whose name was mistakenly thought by the first Spanish invaders to be 'Limac'. This was later shortened slightly to Lima.

Pizarro designed the city, adopting the basic shape of a triangle. It endures as one of the finest examples of Spanish colonial architecture and town planning in South America. Much of its earlier character remains in the form of its stately old plazas and churches, many in the ornate style of the Spanish architect Churriguera. The grandeur of the colonial past culminates in Plaza des Armas, bordered by the presidential palace, the Archbishop's palace, and the cathedral. Interspersed among Lima's fine old buildings are some interesting examples of modern architecture, notably the El Dorada building.

Pisac market, Peru *above*. Come Sunday, the quiet Quechua Indian village of Pisac, set high in the mountains, comes alive with the noise and bustle of the weekly market. Dressed in their Sunday best, wearing panama hats and homburgs, the Indians create a colorful scene. You can buy mementos of the market in the form of antiques, ponchos, highland woollen hats, blankets and local handicrafts. Pisac is also worth visiting for its Inca ruins high above the village.

Peru's rich heritage can be discovered in Lima's collection of more than twenty museums, especially in the Museum of Anthropology and Archaeology with its rare mummified remains, pottery, fascinating tapestries and textiles. The highly acclaimed Gold Museum houses exquisite pre-Columbian artifacts.

Leaving the center of Lima, one of the city's most appealing areas can be found in the delightful suburb of Miraflores with its elegant architecture and, as the name suggests, a multitude of picturesque flowering gardens. Close by is Costa Verde, with its golden Pacific shore that remains refreshingly modest in its development.

No trip to Lima is complete without a visit to the legendary Lost City of the Incas – Machu Picchu. To reach it, take the captivating train ride from the ancient Indian city of Cuzco to Machu Picchu's lofty perch

Market in Salvador, Brazil *left*. The major arts and handicrafts center of Brazil can be found in Salvador, capital of Bahia State. Among the city's many markets, the most important is Feira de São Joaquim which operates every day except Sunday. Saturday is the highlight of the week; the market fills with locals eager to seek out the bargains in fruit and vegetables, some of which are set out on boat stalls along the waterfront. African and Portuguese influences are reflected in the craftwork of pottery, basketware, charms and local musical instruments.

Carnival, Rio de Janeiro *above*. Every year for the five days leading up to Ash Wednesday, Rio de Janeiro is transformed by an explosion of color and music – the hedonistic celebration of 'Carnival'. A sense of anticipation can be felt from as early as November when preparations are begun to make the decorations and costumes that flood the streets during the big event. Sporadic parties occur in the weeks leading up to Carnival, but it is from the Saturday before the beginning of Lent that the party really starts.

some 11,000 feet up in the Andes. In Cuzco visitors can experience the unique Indian culture. Wander around the markets, which brim with life and activity. The pungent aromas of Indian dishes bubbling in huge pots will follow you through the maze of stalls selling almost everything, including exotic herbs and vegetables, intricate basketware and alpaca woollens.

With the Pacific at its doorstep, Lima has a good selection of fish dishes, particularly *corvina* served with a seafood sauce, and *ceviche* – fish soaked in a spicy marinade. Curiously, some of the best Chinese cuisine outside Asia can be found in Lima. However you choose to dine, be sure to precede your meal with a Pisco sour made with grape brandy, fresh limes and egg white.

Escape the US winter and enjoy Lima at its best during its summer months from December through to April.

Copacabana Beach, Rio de Janeiro
right. With such an abundance of
sun and beaches it's little wonder
that visitors and locals alike gravitate
to the beautiful shores of Rio de
Janeiro at every available
opportunity. Copacabana is the
largest and most famous of the
beaches. Its main competition
comes from Ipanema Beach, home
of the diminutive bikini, the tanga. It
is a fashionable area immortalized in
the popular song *Girl from Ipanema*.
Whichever you choose you can't fail
to enjoy Rio's golden sands and
playful atmosphere.

**Bahiana street vendor, Sao Paulo
Brazil** *below.* Remaining serene
amidst Sao Paulo's frenetic pace of
life, this Bahian woman shows the
splendor of her national costume.
Originally of African descent, the
Bahians come from Salvador. Well-
known for their friendliness and
relaxed nature, Bahians can often be
found in the market areas of Brazil's
major cities selling their delicious
acarajé – golden fritters made from
ground beans and fried in oil from
the dende palm.

The Spaniard Pedro de Mendoza first established a city on the banks of the Río de la Plata (River Plate) in 1536, calling the city Nuestra Santa María del Buen Aire (Our Lady Saint Mary of the Good Air). Happily the city's name has since been abbreviated to Buenos Aires and, despite its vast growth, it still retains the 'good air.'

Walk down one of the beautiful wide boulevards in Buenos Aires and you could be forgiven for thinking that you are in Europe. Indeed Buenos Aires is acclaimed as the 'Paris of South America' and emulates much of the style and character of that city; it even has a towering obelisk that is reminiscent of the Eiffel Tower. The avenues and boulevards have a French look to them which contrasts strikingly with their blossoming jacarandas and acacia trees. In the city's gracious residential areas, rambling mansions and apartment blocks with flower-bedecked balconies are interspersed with some of the many tranquil parks for which Buenos Aires is noted.

The city today is the result of much immigration from Europe. Experience the Bohemian French ambience in the sidewalk cafés, browse through the many stylish art galleries or enjoy the rhythm of the nightlife – remember the tango originated in Argentina. Alternatively the Italian quarter along the waterfront, known locally as La Boca (The Mouth), is full of boisterous cantinas where waiters sing operatically while serving your pasta. By contrast the Hotel Claridge with its English atmosphere and elegant surroundings is extremely genteel; it also affords some of the finest accommodation and cuisine in Buenos Aires.

The arts play a prominent part in the pattern of life in Buenos Aires. There are opportunities to enjoy open-air theater, amateur dramatics or professional opera and concerts at the Colon Theater.

The Plaza de Mayo, where Argentina's independence from Spain was first planned, is still the heart and life of Buenos Aires. It is dominated by the presidential palace, known as the Pink House, and the cathedral where San Martin, one of the liberators of South America from Spanish rule, is buried. Near to the plaza runs Avenue 9th July, one of the longest and widest streets in the world. Competing with its grandeur is the Calle Florida, a fashionable pedestrian precinct with exclusive shops and boutiques such as 'Harrods B.A.'

Although Argentina has a fine selection of seafood the favorite at nearly every meal is its famous steak. A typical restaurant meal is the *parillada mixta* (mixed grill). The cuisine is complemented by a wide variety of local wines.

An elegant, vivacious city, Buenos Aires offers the visitor a taste of Europe which is distinctly Latin American.

Avenida 9th July and Obelisk, Buenos Aires *left.* Commemorating the day in 1816 when Argentina gained full independence from Spain, the Avenida 9th July is a grand boulevard, one of the widest in the world (425 feet). Lined with cafés, its allure is reminiscent of the grand streets of Paris and it is a popular haunt of shoppers and those seeking to relax with a coffee or cocktail. Rising some 70 feet above the boulevard stands the Obelisk, a favorite subject for holiday snapshots. Surrounded by lawns dotted with flowerbeds, the Obelisk marks the intersection with the Calle Corrientes, Buenos Aires' nightlife area. The two enormous fountains in Avenida 9th July are best seen at night. They provide an elaborate display of water which is visible for several blocks. With all these attractions, it is not surprising that this has become a popular place for strolling in, and that perennial pastime, 'people-watching'.

TRAVEL TIPS

Although each of the South American countries have individual traits there are some general rules for prospective travelers which apply to all. A valid US passport and, frequently, a visa are required. Travelers should take health precautions by seeking advice on inoculations from their physician. Always avoid drinking the local water. Although some people in large resorts will speak English, it is essential to take phrase books: Spanish in Argentina and Peru, Portuguese in Brazil.

Tipping varies between countries, with restaurants in Peru accepting 10% whereas in Argentina and Brazil, although service charges are included in the bill, a further 15% tip is expected. Banks are usually open from 10:00 am to 4:00 pm, but they are only open in the mornings in Peru. Peru's taxis have no meters so fares are determined before starting. Brazil and Argentina both have metered taxi fares.

The best time to travel to South America is from December to April – during the summer months. While South America is a photographer's paradise, remember that certain Indian tribes do not wish to be photographed, and will be upset if you attempt to do so.

South America's legal systems vary considerably from those in North America. It is well worth carrying identification at all times, and contacting the United States' Consulate in the event of any legal problems. It is common in the case of a road accident for all parties to be detained until the incident is resolved, so endeavour to pay for any liability on the spot.

Argentinian gauchos *above.* The gauchos of the Argentine grasslands followed a nomadic existence during the 18th and 19th centuries. Noted for their riding skills, today's gauchos still dress in the striking style of their cowboy forebears.

Congresso Square, Buenos Aires *far left.* Dominating Congresso Square stands the stately white edifice of the National Congress Building. The neo-classical design with its fine columns is reminiscent of ancient Greek and Roman architecture. The square, which is a popular place for the locals to pass their time, features impressive statues and a grand fountain. Situated at the end of the Avenida de Mayo, the enormous Congress Building occupies an entire block. It is the center and forum for Argentina's government and has been a focal point in much of the country's passionate political past.

Iguasu Falls, Brazil *left.* At the point where the borders of Brazil, Paraguay and Argentina converge lie the Iguasu Falls. These are the largest waterfalls in the world, far surpassing Niagara and Victoria Falls. From a distance of several miles the thunderous roar of the mammoth torrents can be heard, building to a deafening roar as you approach. The falls are fed by the combined waters of the Paranapanema, Paraná and Iguasu Rivers that flow through lush jungle. The falls can be seen from a variety of viewpoints, including helicopters, walkways and boats.

Index

Acknowledgements

The publishers thank the following for providing the photographs in this book:
The Photo Source/CLI 2–3, 6–7, 14, 17, 18–19, 22–23, 26 right, 30–31, 32, 33, 34 above, 40–41, 45 below, 47, 49, 58, 63 above; Zefa Picture Library 1, 4–5, 8–9, 10–11, 11, 12, 13, 14–15, 15, 16, 19, 20, 20–21, 22, 23, 24–25, 26 left, 27, 28–29, 34 below, 35, 36, 37, 38, 39, 42–43, 44, 45 above, 46, 48, 48–49, 50–51, 52–53, 54, 55, 56–57, 57, 58–59, 60–61, 62, 63 below.